# BOSS RULES

THE FIRST 25 STEPS
TO INSPIRE YOU
FORWARD

SHARAKA M. LEONARD

Copyright © 2020 by Sharaka M. Leonard
All rights reserved. Printed in the United States of America. No parts of this book may be used, reproduced, duplicated, or transmitted in any manner whatsoever without written permission except in the case of brief quotations embodied in critical articles or reviews.

For more information contact:
info@shepublishingllc.com
www.shepublishingllc.com


ISBNs:
Paperback (*matte*):  978-1-7350327-8-8
Paperback (*gloss*):  978-1-7350327-9-5
Hardcover:  978-1-953163-00-4


First Edition: October 2020

S.H.E. PUBLISHING, LLC

10 9 8 7 6 5 4 3 2 1

# CONTENTS

INTRODUCTION ................................................................................ VII

BOSS RULE 1: STAY CURIOUS AND BE A PROBLEM SOLVER ................ 3

BOSS RULE 2: SAY LESS THAN OTHERS AROUND YOU ........................ 5

BOSS RULE 3: LISTEN WITH YOUR HEART, NOT JUST YOUR HEAD . 7

BOSS RULE 4: THINK BEFORE YOU REACT ........................................ 9

BOSS RULE 5: PIMP YOURSELF—DON'T LET ANYBODY PIMP YOU .. 11

BOSS RULE 6: GIVE MORE THAN YOU RECEIVE ............................... 13

BOSS RULE 7: BE WILLING TO MOVE AHEAD ALONE— EVERYBODY'S NOT BUILT FOR BEGINNINGS ................................... 15

BOSS RULE 8: ACTION BEATS TALK EVERY TIME ............................ 17

BOSS RULE 9: YOU'RE GOING TO DO DISTASTEFUL THINGS ON YOUR RIDE TO SUCCESS ................................................................. 19

BOSS RULE 10: BE READY, STAY READY, AND MOVE WITH INTENT 21

BOSS RULE 11: AGILITY WINS MORE THAN ATTITUDE ................... 23

BOSS RULE 12: EVERYBODY CAN TEACH YOU SOMETHING ........... 25

BOSS RULE 13: PLAN ON THINGS GOING AWRY, AND HAVE A PLAN FOR THE PLAN ............................................................................... 27

BOSS RULE 14: TURN YOUR THINKING DOWN AND YOUR FAITH UP ................................................................................................... 29

BOSS RULE 15: MULTITASK EVERY CHANCE YOU GET TO MAXIMIZE EFFORTS ...................................................................... 31

BOSS RULE 16: WHEN IT'S POPPING, MILK IT—WHEN IT'S NOT, LEAVE IT ALONE..................................................................................33

BOSS RULE 17: FAIL FABULOUSLY, AND FLEX ON THEM NEXT TIME ...............................................................................................................35

BOSS RULE 18: RUN YOUR RACE WITH YOUR EYES AHEAD................37

BOSS RULE 19: GET AND STAY ASSERTIVE ................................................. 39

BOSS RULE 20: LOVE YOURSELF ENOUGH TO PRACTICE WELLNESS ................................................................................................................41

BOSS RULE 21: NEVER LET YOUR LEFT HAND KNOW YOUR RIGHT HAND'S MOVES........................................................................................ 43

BOSS RULE 22: FAIL BIG AND FAIL OFTEN ................................................. 45

BOSS RULE 23: MISS ME ALL THE DRAMA, CHASE COMMAS ............ 47

BOSS RULE 24: BE YOUR OWN CHEERLEADER ........................................ 49

BOSS RULE 25: PEOPLE HEAR BUT DON'T LISTEN—SAVE YOUR BREATH ..................................................................................................... 51

ACKNOWLEDGMENTS .................................................................................. 55

AFTERWORD .................................................................................................... 56

PULSE CHECK .................................................................................................. 58

MINIGOAL CHALLENGE................................................................................ 60

THREE-YEAR GOAL ........................................................................................ 61

- VS - .................................................................................................................... 61

FIVE-YEAR GOAL CHALLENGE ................................................................... 61

TWENTY-BY-FIVE CHALLENGE .................................................................. 62

*Don't get angry. Don't get revenge.*

*Get moving. Get strategic.*

*Move toward the success you deserve.*

*If they are not on your page, turn it.*

*If they are not on your level, step up.*

*If they are not part of the plan, ignore them.*

—Sharaka M. Leonard

# INTRODUCTION

Bosses aren't born: they are made. They are made out of desperation, aggravation, and an unwillingness to conform. As a worker bee all my life until now, I chose that life; now I am choosing something else. I choose to be the boss of myself, my choices, and my life. I choose to pursue my passion and purpose with the same resilience I have shown employers over the last twenty years.

A boss mindset is how you perceive and maneuver through the world. I found myself humble enough to lead my own path, break new ground, and be the change I wanted to see. Taking calculated risks more frequently got me where I wanted to be faster. You are the boss of your life: you can promote people within your life, you can fire them, or you can send them on a leave of absence as you see fit. If it doesn't bring you one of the three M's (money, meaning, or more knowledge), it doesn't belong in your life. Use these rules to be the boss of your own life and make boss moves.

# BOSS 1 RULE

-> BOSS RULES <-

# Boss Rule 1: Stay Curious and Be a Problem Solver

How many people leave it at "I don't know" and stop? Their thinking is diverted to the next thing, and yet the problem still remains. If no solution has been provided, then you be the solution. Even if the impact is small, your initiative to get to the bottom of things is valued by your employer. It is valued by friends and family. In day-to-day life, throwing your hands up and saying "it is what it is" solves nothing.

What can you do? Stay curious and ask yourself, "Why? Why am I doing it this way? Why is this way the best?" If you cannot come up with a good enough reason, make a change. You will find that you have solved not only your own problems, but the problems of others. Your value and worth just went up. You have become the go-to person; you are now a subject matter expert (SME). Find what interests you, then find out how to make money off it.

-> SHARAKA M. LEONARD <-

# BOSS RULE 2

# Boss Rule 2: Say Less Than Others Around You

How many times do you hear people tip toe around a subject instead of getting to the point? Observe and listen; learn the signs and expressions of the people around you. Most people love to talk, so let them. Read the room. Being a good listener will help you later. If you are silent, you can be observant. You can plot and plan to move your way to the top. If you use it correctly, silence can serve as a defense and an offense.

Do not be the loudest voice in the room. It is annoying and shows that you are trying too hard. You can command the room with brief and concise statements. Leave something to be desired. Being long winded and repeating yourself shows self-absorption and a lack of knowledge. Keep your thoughts to yourself until talking about them can reap the most benefits.

-> SHARAKA M. LEONARD <-

# BOSS RULE 3

# Boss Rule 3: Listen with Your Heart, Not Just Your Head

Be nice to folks. Not every move is a money move. Your time and your care are just as valuable as your business. Do not lose your humanity in the adventure to be a boss. You are just as worthy as the next person, and being kind is not a weakness.

To listen with your heart is to be open to where the other person is coming from. This means not letting your head cloud your ability to hear the other person. You can psychoanalyze it later for the lesson, but to listen initially with a humble and open heart as well as an open mind only enriches you.

-> SHARAKA M. LEONARD <-

# BOSS RULE 4

# Boss Rule 4: Think before You React

Remember that to take action is to show purpose. You should only act when you have a precise intent and a goal to achieve, even if that intent is to change minds. Weigh the consequences, and remove the emotion. Not all reactions have to be at "that" moment in time. Sometimes you can walk away, reset, then gather yourself. Then, bust a move. That move can be swift, or it can be timed.

People say and do things without thinking. Be different: be rebellious and think before you act. Strategy is the difference between a boss and an employee. Planning is the key, and execution is the door. Kick it open and make yourself heard, now. Make your vision crystal clear. Know that you can modify it along the way, but stay steadfast in your conviction and belief in what you want to do.

-> SHARAKA M. LEONARD <-

# BOSS RULE 5

## Boss Rule 5: Pimp Yourself— Don't Let Anybody Pimp You

If you have to have a label, then pick your own brand, oversee your brand, and direct yourself. You can brand yourself as the efficient one, the thorough one, the problem solver, or something else with a positive connotation. Do not let anyone label you or box you in. Set the standard and force those around you to acknowledge it. Just be assertive: remain unbothered. Do not be a jerk; be well positioned. If someone must call you a name, then you dictate the terms. Make sure there is a "Ms./Mr." or a "Boss" in front of all names somebody else wishes to scream out.

If I must work for someone else, I want to work on my own terms, knowing I am respected, treated fairly, and valued for my contributions. Not all workplaces allow for this kind of environment. Find a place that does allow for this, or create your own utopia. It's time for boss moves. Seek equality and equity from every situation or deal. If you don't stand up for yourself, no one else will.

-> SHARAKA M. LEONARD <-

# BOSS RULE 6

# Boss Rule 6: Give More Than You Receive

Only by giving of yourself do you attempt to reach your life's purpose. We are all here to be of service: to be of use and to help each other along. I choose to give my time and knowledge. I choose to listen as much as I can to others. I learn something in the mix, and I solidify myself as a loyal friend. It is the cheapest thing to give and builds great karma. Giving is how we balance this world. The slightest effort can come back to you tenfold. Share your time, knowledge, and money when you can.

Giving means there is no thought of "What is in it for me?" You give to help others freely. You give because it is the right thing to do and you want to impact others. You give because you wish someone would have done it for you. I am being the change I want to see, and maybe that change can be contagious. Pay the giving forward.

-> SHARAKA M. LEONARD <-

# BOSS 7 RULE

# Boss Rule 7: Be Willing to Move Ahead Alone—Everybody's Not Built for Beginnings

Many people are Johnny-come-latelies. They are not prepared for the struggle, the research, or the risk; they simply want to come on board once your strategy is working and fruitful. Knowing human nature as I do, you may offer to let them in early. You know their response will be to take no action, so later when you actually succeed, you don't feel guilty. You can shun those doubters and keep moving forward toward your next goal.

People are reluctant in good circumstances, let alone unknown ones. But I firmly believe to have what you have never had; you have to do what you have never done. Only the meek inherit the earth, and I want the freedom to move about the earth and do what I want, when I want, on my own terms. That takes money and power. You may start alone, but you don't have to end that way. Get moving.

-> SHARAKA M. LEONARD <-

# BOSS RULE 8

# Boss Rule 8: Action Beats Talk Every Time

Sitting on their hands never made anyone richer. Plan your attack and gradually see it through. Do not just jump in without any research or inquiries. One of my best friends inspired me by being a doer and not just a talker. My friend took action and never looked back. That courage—that conviction—is to be commended and celebrated by all of us dreamers. She made a boss decision with the fearless pursuit of being her authentic self. I immediately decided to finish my two works in progress for release in 2020 and 2021.

People often want to join you at the top. They want exclusive access, to use the elevator, and to shine in your light. They do not want to build the steps, makes the trips, experience the falls, and help move you closer to the goal post. Most people are reactive and looking for the quickest and easiest way. Sometimes later never comes, so do it now.

-> SHARAKA M. LEONARD <-

# BOSS RULE 9

## Boss Rule 9: You're Going to Do Distasteful Things on Your Ride to Success

Yes, you will have to bite your tongue. Turn the other cheek. Endure annoying people and hear things you don't want to hear. It is a part of life. You do what you must until you are capable of walking away from that situation and standing on your own. You cannot falter when faced with doing things you simply don't want to do to move ahead. This time is temporary, and the end results will outweigh the difficulties of the present.

You must remember that the means justify the ends and to see the bigger picture. If you give in to all of the nonsense along the way or let it make you bitter or mean, then they won and you lost. When others set the tone or control the environment, you play along. Be among them, but not of them. You must have tough skin and know that you have to get a little dirty and messed up to achieve your goals.

-> SHARAKA M. LEONARD <-

# BOSS RULE 10

## Boss Rule 10: Be Ready, Stay Ready, and Move with Intent

The worst thing about an opportunity is missing out on one because you were unable to participate. Your money wasn't right, you didn't have the time, or you didn't have the look. Be optimistic and know that an opportunity does not have any one person's name on it. You should always think ahead and surround yourself with the right people so that a chance can even appear in front of you. There is no shame in taking advantage of your strategic planning. Plan in advance, so when the time is right, it's not luck—it's your preparedness—that allows you to partake in the opportunity.

I believe in always having goals, both small and gigantic. If you continue to push yourself to stay ready, you will be ready for anything that comes your way. I started investing with $100 dollars on my Robinhood app. In five months, I grew it to $3,000. I started buying gold and silver coins when others were buying frivolous items. I did it incrementally and with whatever extra cash came my way. I moved with intent because I knew that only I could protect myself and that only I could see that things always do change. You are either going to be proactive or reactive in your life.

-> SHARAKA M. LEONARD <-

# BOSS RULE 11

# Boss Rule 11: Agility Wins More Than Attitude

You have to be fluid with your responses to those around you. You cannot show fear, anger, doubt, or disgust. You have to remain professional and smile while you claw your way to the top. Like the old saying goes, you get further with honey than you do with vinegar. Snapping back would be satisfactory in the moment. But what about all the moments after? You can bite your tongue temporarily until you get the power and prestige that lets you dictate the rules.

You can play dumb; just don't actually be dumb. Be the boss of your emotions and make an executive decision. You will not cave. Agility of mind means you can see in multiple dimensions and you can react fast to the changes around you when needed. You are the inventor of your destiny and your path. There is no right or wrong path, only what did work and what didn't work on your journey. Let the findings of this experiment guide you in the next direction.

-> SHARAKA M. LEONARD <-

# BOSS RULE 12

# Boss Rule 12: Everybody Can Teach You Something

Even the most unlikely person can provide insight, if you listen intently. Don't turn away from the source; use all sources as a fountain of knowledge. You can learn lessons on what to do and what not to do. Be humble in your receipt of the information and apply as needed. Be aware that inspiration and information can come from anyone you encounter. Keep your eyes and mind open to find opportunities in all the information you obtain.

Learn from others' mistakes. Learn from others' successes. See where you fit in on the scale and deviate as needed. Open-mindedness does not mean you take in and process all of the information; only pull out the piece or pieces that fit your agenda. Observations are gifts; they allow you to see beyond what the person is putting in front of your face. People wear masks. People tell lies. You can see a mistake and pivot. Watch, listen, and learn from others.

-> SHARAKA M. LEONARD <-

# BOSS RULE 13

# Boss Rule 13: Plan on Things Going Awry, and Have a Plan for the Plan

Nothing goes as planned, so have a plan B, a plan C, and a plan D. Know that people are involved and are fallible. People disappoint. People fall short, and you're not perfect either. There is always something you missed, didn't get quite right, or thought was correct at the time but realized otherwise later. Knowing yourself and others allows you to plan ahead cautiously. Having this set up means that if you have to jump ship, you have two life boats on opposite sides to keep you afloat.

Move like chess masters do. See the possibilities in the next three, five, or ten steps. You can never overplan in my opinion. I look at it like platforms. Build three platforms; if one collapses, you simply jump to the next one and you never have to start from scratch again. Why? Because you built multiple steps to stand on. Think several steps ahead, and you'll never be caught slipping.

-> SHARAKA M. LEONARD <-

# BOSS RULE 14

# Boss Rule 14: Turn Your Thinking Down and Your Faith Up

I believe I speak things into existence. I think of an aspiration and sometimes, I think so much about it, I talk myself right out making a move on it. I think too much and too hard and nothing gets finished. With that said, think and let be. Write it down in a journal, make a vision board, and or just put a sticky note on your wall. You did step 1, you thought about it. Step 2 is the faith that it will happen. Step 3 is the action to support steps 1 and 2.

Mental wellness is equally important as physical wellness. You have to believe in yourself and GOD, a higher power to get to the next level. "There is a breakthrough in the room with your name on it," as Tasha Cobb says. You have to step back and let your choice of higher power move over and through your discovery. We think it is just us that make things happen. That is untrue.

-> SHARAKA M. LEONARD <-

# BOSS RULE 15

# Boss Rule 15: Multitask Every Chance You Get to Maximize Efforts

Do you know that I am not idle by nature? If I am working at my regular job, I am also thinking about side hustles. If I am walking, I may take exaggerated steps to strengthen my legs and add arm movements to work my lower and upper body at the same time. I am intentionally upping my movements to get more done at the same time and stay flexible. If I am standing in a line somewhere, I am doing butt lifts or toe raises to get a jump on a workout I may or may not do later. The point is that I am doing multiple things at one time, always. I cannot stop moving.

I do this to maximize my efforts. Why? Because, why put off later what you can do right now. It's the best example of not wasting time that I have ever engaged in. Try it next time. I may do sit ups during commercials, practice meditation breathing exercise while walking the dog, or even leg lifts and arm curls while on a Zoom call. There is no reason we cannot accomplish something. There is always time; just use it more wisely.

-> SHARAKA M. LEONARD <-

# BOSS RULE 16

## Boss Rule 16: When It's Popping, Milk It—When It's Not, Leave It Alone

When things are good, jump on the opportunities they provide; do not delay or wait. For example, you find a stock price at a low $5 per share. You do your research and see that there is government funding approved for this, or that a merger is pending, or that this company could change an industry. You have $100 to invest. Would you invest your entire $100, or would you only invest $20? Most would be skeptical and only invest the minimum. But no risk, no gain. You have to see an opportunity in front of you and make the best financial decision. You have to strike while the iron is hot or lose it when it cools down.

Nothing lasts forever; however, regrets do last for a lifetime. Who knows how many opportunities fall into your lap or how often? Missing the mark when things are at the pinnacle and then going in hard when you're in the valley is very counterproductive. Today, you see your favorite celebrity on top; the next time, they disappear. When you're on a roll, make the most of it, because it will come to a halt. While you were popping, did you set yourself up for the future? Did you make the relationships or plans for when it all goes silent?

-> SHARAKA M. LEONARD <-

# BOSS RULE 17

# Boss Rule 17: FAIL Fabulously, and Flex on Them Next Time

Every door that closes in your face is a chance to kick down another door, go through the basement, or crawl through a window: don't go down without a fight, and do learn from the experience. I am my own worst enemy. Take paying bills, for example. You know the due date and the amount, yet you wait until the last minute to pay it on the due date. But now it's after hours, so the payment has tomorrow's date instead of todays. You just gave away money as a late fee, for nothing. Next time pay it two days earlier—even if it drains your account—so you're not paying extra for no good reason.

If everything went your way, how would you improve? Sometimes that "no" can set a fire within you. Hearing "there's nothing we can do" can make you upset. Hearing that "we're going to go in another direction" makes you want to move in new ways and accomplish more than if you had heard a "yes" at that time. FAIL just means *Figured-Out Another Incredible Lesson.*

-> SHARAKA M. LEONARD <-

# BOSS RULE

# Boss Rule 18: Run Your Race With Your Eyes Ahead

I don't like having blinders on. I like running my race and seeing what's going on in my peripheral view. I need to see what's happening around me; I can glance not stare. Knowing where you are in your race is an advantage and should be used to the best of your ability. When you do this, you don't care about placement or medals, because your race is a singular competition. You care about the journey and the results, whether you complete the race or not.

If the journey was not bumpy, would you really appreciate the destination once you arrived? I think not. We tend to get hung up on the irrelevant obstacles we come across and shortchange ourselves on a full sense of achievement when we have done what we set out to do or gone where we set out to go. Keeping your eyes ahead means you can run your race and adjust your pace if needed. Who doesn't look both ways before crossing the street? You know the other knuckleheads could be going the wrong way and on a slant. You have to see them to know to jump or duck. It doesn't mean you take your eyes off the ball; you just have to heighten your sense of awareness.

-> SHARAKA M. LEONARD <-

# BOSS RULE 19

# Boss Rule 19: Get and Stay Assertive

The goal rarely changes, but the path might. You have to create the path yourself, take the initiative to research and review those who did it first. The how may be standard, but your why makes all the difference. I've always believed that closed mouths don't get fed. Ask for the world and maybe you'll get what you deserve. Say nothing, and you cannot complain. This applies to being a boss. Ask for the moon, you just might get stars. You never know what others may say yes to until you ask. Someone else may have the same thought or point of view, and you can build a business relationship based on that.

Take a calculated risk on yourself. Be brief and concise. Close mouths don't get fed, and nobody is itching to hand you anything for free. Once you begin asking, don't stop; make reasonable asks that can be delivered and that make life better for more people than just yourself. When you get others to buy in, it's hard to say no. This life is hard, and it's miserable for those who don't assert themselves. Be seen by, be heard by, and be relevant to those you interact with. Be memorable.

-> SHARAKA M. LEONARD <-

# BOSS RULE 20

## Boss Rule 20: Love Yourself Enough to Practice Wellness

Celebrate the small wins and even the failures you experience. This means taking care of yourself mentally and physically. No dream can be realized if you are not there to see it and enjoy it. You are the biggest asset to your dream. You are the biggest investment and investor. This includes participating in meditation, turning your phone off, getting a massage, going into seclusion, and disconnecting from the world.

Let people wonder where you are. Refresh your mind and body from time to time. Seek clarity and inspiration from solitude and silence. It's necessary and mandatory. Disconnect from time to time. Unplug and unwind with a clear head and relaxed body. Take a "me day." It's okay; you're not missing anything that will not be there when you return.

-> SHARAKA M. LEONARD <-

# BOSS RULE 21

# Boss Rule 21: Never Let Your Left Hand Know Your Right Hand's Moves

Today people overshare. They talk too much and use too much fluff. You only need to relay the high-level details; be as ambiguous as you can be and even nonchalant. People will zoom in on your revelation and give you all types of poor advice. Do not soak it in; instead, be a collector. Collect all of their important information, then dispose the rest as waste. Move in silence. Let everyone else brag and speak about their moves. You keep yours to yourself.

Your left hand is going here, but your right hand is going there; they do not have to share their objectives. You can have more than one thing going on at a time. It's nobody's business but your own for now. Keep your ideas to yourself initially. Wait for when you have built trust and the friendship is equally balanced. When you speak out about your intentions, you could inspire others to use your thoughts and ideas to advance their own agenda. Move strategically and say less; share less, and see if you don't accomplish more.

-> SHARAKA M. LEONARD <-

# BOSS RULE 22

# Boss Rule 22: FAIL Big and FAIL Often

FAIL can mean your *Finding All Incorrect Lessons*— it's all about perspectives. You don't have to associate negativity with the word FAIL. It doesn't have to break you or upset you. Instead, pause and recognize that your approach didn't work. Okay, roger that — don't do it that way again and move forward. Ask yourself, "What can I try next? What did I learn from this?" Having this attitude will make you a happier and healthier individual.

Sometimes we defeat ourselves. We think that because no one is pointing out a flaw or a failure, something has got to be wrong. We seek the negative in many things because that is what we are conditioned to do. It's time to reprogram yourself to see the win in fail. When we fail, rethink what fail means. FAIL = *First Attempt In Learning*. Fail forward. Fail over and over until you get it right. I would rather fail at reaching for something so big, than to have never tried or started at all. Change your perspective. Find the opportunity for growth in all fails. There are silver linings even in a failure.

-> SHARAKA M. LEONARD <-

# BOSS RULE 23

# Boss Rule 23: Miss Me All the Drama, Chase Commas

People talk. People act. You cannot control any of this, but you can control your reaction to it. You cannot lose yourself in the chaos and confusion of others. This is a devil tactic to distract you and delay your success. You have to see these things for what they are: miserable people committing desperate acts that you don't have to address or spend energy on. In corporate America, I notice how everybody is familiar with what is not part of their jobs, but very few know what is part of their jobs. These experiences teach us to sidestep the bull crap and keep moving.

Drama is heavy; it can weigh you down, occupying your thoughts inside and outside of the office. Live with the determination to be the driver of your life. You can do this. Being captain of your own ship, you have to separate your emotions from your logical approach. Focus on your target, don't go astray, stop being reactive, and just be selective.

-> SHARAKA M. LEONARD <-

# BOSS RULE 24

# Boss Rule 24: Be Your Own Cheerleader

Ninety-nine percent of people do not want the best for you, and they don't even want the best for themselves. They want you beneath them, sharing all your woes and grievances. It makes them feel better and more in balance within the world. So how can you expect them to cheer you on toward your goals and dreams? You cannot, and it's unfair to expect them to. They can give support, listen to you, and pat you on the back, but a cheerleader is motivating and deliberate.

Cheerleaders hype you up even when you're losing. They don't lose the energy knowing the hope of a winning outcome. So, I decided to be my own cheerleader, loudly cheering myself up after a fall or after I stopped or oozing positivity, when negativity threatened to engulf me like a black cloud. I became my own revelation: that I am a boss and should act accordingly.

# BOSS RULE 25

# Boss Rule 25: People Hear but Don't Listen—Save Your Breath

Stop talking to know-it-alls. Find people who are open-minded and open to listening to others as well as sharing their own thoughts. I can't stand it when someone cannot answer a direct question, probably because it has never dawned on them to think of it. When you think you have it all mapped out, you're usually waiting on something, not actively building your presence, brand, or plan. If you cannot think backward and forward about why you are on your particular path, then you cannot clearly articulate your thoughts and vision. You will never be as great as you think you are already.

I am a student of people; I use people for what they are good for. Some people are good to share thoughts with; others aren't. Know whom you are dealing with and treat them accordingly; you will rarely be surprised or disappointed. Test them: hit them with something small and see how they react. People will reveal their limitations in no time. Continue to deal with them or drop them like dead weight.

*SWAG Your Goals*

*Speak it*

*Work at it*

*Analyze it*

*Go at it again*

—Sharaka M. Leonard

-> BOSS RULES <-

*I always knew I was great; I just didn't know which path in life would get me there.*

—Sharaka M. Leonard

-> SHARAKA M. LEONARD <-

# ACKNOWLEDGMENTS

First, thanks to God for being my creative foundation and canvas. This book is a culmination of years of life experiences that has shaped me into the author I am today.

Special thanks to S.H.E. Publishing, LLC and Elite Authors for collaborating in assisting to complete this project. Our collaboration has been a true partnership and learning experience I will never forget.

I'd like to express genuine gratitude and appreciation to my family and friends for their unwavering suppport.

Sharaka M. Leonard

# AFTERWORD

There are three types of people:

1.) People who "fake" got you.
Question when it benefits them.

2.) People who got you "regardless."
No questions need to be asked.

3.) People who got you "messed up."
Question with no purpose.

    The truth about betrayal is that it comes from your closest friend, never your enemy: enemies respect you more and don't underestimate you. Since I cannot be everything to everybody, I choose to be me and I accept all my strengths and weakness equally. I look at myself as living art; I may not suit the taste of all, but I am a rarity to a few.

    Thanks for being open-minded and reading these theories that I have developed over my lifetime. I hope they give you a different perspective on how you can make boss moves right now. There is no need to wait. I am open and available for feedback and consultation. I can be the cheerleader in your life, if you choose. Sign up for one-on-one consultations.

**Other Services:**

- Email for an appointment: **bossrules2020@gmail.com**
- Let me hear your favorite rule and why
- Customized vision board
- One-on-one cheerleading consult (email your answers from the Pulse Check survey)

If you enjoyed this book and want to take the next steps, try the Pulse Check survey on your own and see where you stand right now. Reach out to me for further consultations so we can discuss your ambitions and create a plan for implementation.

# PULSE CHECK

*Let me learn about you...*

1. Why do you enjoy your life?

2. What value do you bring to others and the world?

3. What is the best thing about being you?

4. What is your greatest trait?

5. What is your worst trait?

6. Are you happy with where you are in life?

7. Could life be better now? If so, how?

8. What are you passionate about?

9. If you had to choose between physical health and mental wealth, which would you choose?

10. If you could slowly save $500,000 or receive $100,000 now, which would you prefer?

11. If you had to lose some friends, family, or bad habits, could you to achieve success in your life?

12. Do you view the world as out to get you or as full of opportunity?

13. What skill do you have or want to develop for your business?

14. Which rules make it into your top five and why?

15. If you could have your own private cheerleader, would you pay for this service?

The next steps are up to you. The following pages contain a few worksheets to help you make the next choice.

# MINIGOAL CHALLENGE

*Goals you can accomplish in 12 months or less:*

1.

2.

3.

4.

5.

# THREE-YEAR GOAL
## - VS -
# FIVE-YEAR GOAL CHALLENGE

*Really believable goals and aspirations you want to achieve in each time frame:*

1.

2.

3.

4.

5.

---

1.

2.

3.

4.

5.

# TWENTY-BY-FIVE CHALLENGE

This challenge of choosing twenty things in each of these five groups will allow you to think outside of the box and confront yourself when you ask, "What do I really want?" It's easy to rattle off two or three items, but to list twenty is a test. You will really get to know yourself, and then you can develop yourself to be the best boss you can be. On the next page, please find a few examples from my personal list. Review them and explore what your answers may be.

Sometimes we trap ourselves in our thoughts on what is far fetched, or out of reach, within our lives. This exercise will challenge you to think critically, to stretch yourself, and to image the possibilities. If you can think it, you can envision it and then you can attain it. It's within your power to manifest your destiny.

| FUN THINGS | PERSONAL IMPROVEMENT | CONTRIBUTION/LEGACY | FINANCIAL/BUSINESS | RELATIONSHIP |
|---|---|---|---|---|
| Learn how to pilot a plane | Read a book per month | Open a non-profit dance studio | Purchase 1st building by a (3 - flat) | Be a Foster Parent to kids |
| Visit every island in the caribbean | Lose 40 pounds by end of this year | Non-profit for young women | Becoming a Life coach | Be kind to more people |
| Learn how to sail a boat | Win an award | Donate to a charity for animals | Be worth 45 million by age 45 | Make 3 new friends |
| | | | | |
| | | | | |
| | | | | |
| | | | | |
| | | | | |
| | | | | |
| | | | | |
| | | | | |
| | | | | |
| | | | | |
| | | | | |
| | | | | |
| | | | | |
| | | | | |
| 17 items left | 17 items left | 17 items left | 17 items left | 17 items left |

# Chart Details from Prior Page

## Column 1: Fun things

Pick twenty things that you want to do or learn that are just fun.

## Column 2: Personal Improvement

Improving yourself is ongoing, so pick twenty things that you would like to improve upon.

## Column 3: Contribution/Legacy

We want to leave this world better than we found it, so what twenty things can you to contribute?

## Column 4: Financial/Business

The average millionaire has at least seven streams of income. I challenge you to find twenty.

## Column 5: Relationships

You are not an island and cannot be successful alone. Find ways to improve your relationships with others.

www.ingramcontent.com/pod-product-compliance
Lightning Source LLC
Chambersburg PA
CBHW050507240426
43673CB00004B/139